Genesis 37 verses 5–9

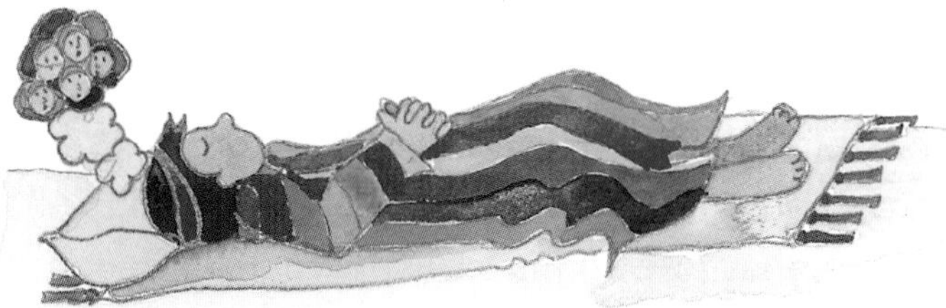

One day Joseph had some dreams and he told them to his brothers. 'In the dreams that I had,' said Joseph, 'you are all bowing down to me.'
The brothers were even more cross with Joseph!

Talkabout

Do you have dreams? Can you tell someone about them?

Prayer

Dear Jesus, I know You are with me when I have dreams in the night whether they are nice or scary. Amen

Sold off

Genesis 37 verses 27–28

So the brothers decided to get rid of Joseph. They sold him to some passing people going to Egypt. But before handing Joseph over to them they tore off his beautiful coat and kept it.

Talkabout

How do you think Joseph felt after his brothers had done this?

Prayer

Dear Lord, even though this was horrible for Joseph ... thank You for being with him. Amen

Jesus and Me Every Day

Eira Reeves

Book 3

Published 2010 by CWR, Waverley Abbey House, Waverley Lane, Farnham, Surrey GU9 8EP, UK. Registered Charity No. 294387. Registered Limited Company No. 1990308.

For a list of our National Distributors, visit www.cwr.org.uk

Concept development, editing, design and production by CWR

Printed in Latvia by Yeomans Press

ISBN: 978-1-85345-544-5

CONTENTS

JOSEPH

Day 1

Favourite son

Genesis 37 verse 3

There was a father called Jacob and he had twelve sons. He loved them all. But there was one son, Joseph the shepherd, who was his favourite.

Talkabout

Have you ever noticed anyone being the favourite? What did you think?

Prayer

Thank You, dear Jesus, that You don't have favourites. We are all special to You. Amen

Genesis 37 verse 3

Day 2
A beautiful coat

One day Jacob made a beautiful coat for his favourite son Joseph. The coat had many, many colours. It was SO beautiful when Joseph put it on. 'Don't I just look wonderful!' said Joseph, with a big smile.

Talkabout

What colour clothes do you like to wear and why?

Prayer

Dear Lord, thank You that You give us clothes to wear. Amen

Day 3
Jealous

Genesis 37 verse 4

When Joseph's brothers saw the beautiful coat their father had made for him ... they hated Joseph and were very jealous. They couldn't even speak nicely to Joseph.

Talkabout

Why do you think Joseph's brothers were like this? Look at Day 1.

Prayer

Dear Jesus, please help me never to be jealous or horrible to anyone. Amen

Day 6
A lie

Genesis 37 verses 32–34

The brothers returned to the camp where Jacob their father was sitting.
They showed Joseph's coat to Jacob. 'A wild animal must have killed Joseph,' they said.
Jacob started to cry.

Talkabout

The brothers had told a lie. Have you ever heard anyone not telling the truth?

Prayer

Dear Lord, help me never to tell lies to anyone, only the truth. Amen

Day 7

The best job ever

Genesis 41 verses 40–42

Once in Egypt, Joseph went through some hard times, but God was with him, always helping him – especially when Joseph met Pharaoh, the ruler. Pharaoh became proud of Joseph and he gave him the best job in Egypt! He also gave him a beautiful ring and many smart clothes.

Talkabout

What do you like about this story and why?

Prayer

Thank You, dear God, that You looked after Joseph all through the bad times. Amen

THE LOST SHEEP

Luke 15 verses 1–3

Day **8**

Listen and learn

Jesus loved telling stories to teach people. One day many people gathered around Him as He told a story about a lost sheep. They all listened very carefully.

Talkabout

Do you listen carefully when you are read a story? Can you remember your favourite story?

Dear Jesus, I just love to learn from all Your stories. I promise to try to listen very carefully! Amen

Day 9
Counting

Luke 15 verse 4

There was a shepherd who looked after one hundred sheep. One day the shepherd wanted to count them all to make sure he still had one hundred. As he counted the sheep they were either just standing about or eating grass.

Talkabout

What number can you count up to?

Thank You for shepherds and sheep everywhere, dear Jesus. Please can You take care of them all. Amen

Luke 15 verse 4

Day **10**

One missing

'OH NO,' cried the shepherd after counting, 'there's one sheep missing!' He was so sad. Immediately the shepherd left the other ninety-nine sheep and set off to go and look for the one lost sheep.

Talkabout

Have you ever seen sheep? What do you like about them?

Dear Jesus, thank You for this shepherd who cared about his lost sheep. Amen

Day **11**

Luke 15 verse 4

Searching everywhere

The shepherd searched the hills and over the fields. He shouted and shouted for that one lost sheep. He looked behind bushes and he looked behind rocks. 'Where are you?' he cried.

Talkabout

How do you feel when you have lost something very special?

Dear Jesus, when I have lost something precious to me please help me find it. Amen

Luke 15 verse 5

Day **12**

Found at last!

At last the shepherd saw the lost sheep. 'Thank goodness,' he cried, 'I have found you.' The sheep was glad too! He was so pleased that the shepherd had even bothered to come looking for him when he was lost.

What do you think is important in this story?

Dear Jesus, thank You that You love me like the shepherd loves his sheep. Help me never to wander away from You. Amen

Luke 15 verse 6

Day 13

Everyone is happy!

The shepherd then carried the sheep on his shoulders. He took him all the way back to the flock. He saw his friends on the way and said, 'I have found the lost sheep!'
He was so happy. All his friends were happy too!

Do you like this shepherd? Why?

Dear Jesus, thank You for this story as it reminds me that You are my shepherd and You take care of me. Amen

Day 14

John 12 verse 26

Everywhere with Jesus

Kelly's mummy was reading to her from the Bible. 'I like this verse,' said Mummy. 'Jesus is asking His friends to follow Him.'
Kelly looked up at her mummy, 'I want to follow Jesus too,' she said.

Talkabout Can you say how you would like to follow Jesus?

Please show me, dear Jesus, how I can always follow You. Amen

Day 15
Serve like Jesus

John 12 verse 26

One afternoon Ben helped to collect empty cups from the older people at church having tea. Ben looked up at Mrs White, who was also helping with the teas. 'I want to follow and serve Jesus,' he said, 'and help people like He did.'

Talkabout

'Serve' means to 'help or do something for someone.' How would you like to serve Jesus today?

Prayer

Dear Jesus, please show me each day how to follow and serve You. Amen

John 8 verse 12

Day 16
Light of Jesus

Mummy lit a candle.
The friends watched around the table.
'This light is like Jesus,' said Mummy, 'and Jesus said that if you follow Him you'll always be in His light.'
'Mummy,' said Sue, 'will you help me light a candle too?'

Talkabout

Can you think of ways to follow the light of Jesus?

Dear Jesus, I always want to be in Your light – never let me go. Amen

Day 17
Follow His light

Psalm 119 verse 105

Sue and Max and their daddy were coming home late one night. 'Ooooh, it's very dark,' said Sue, who was a little frightened. 'Don't worry,' said Daddy, 'I have a torch here. It will light our way as we walk along – just as Jesus can light our way.'

How can learning about Jesus help us to see clearly and follow His way?

Dear Jesus, I always want to follow Your light. Amen

Day **18**

Do as you're told!

Deuteronomy 27 verse 10

Kim was busy playing in the garden.
'Kim,' said Daddy, 'please come in for supper now.'
But Kim was a bit naughty, he didn't do as he was told and went on playing in the garden.

Talkabout

What would happen if you didn't follow what Jesus and your parents have asked you to do?

Prayer

Dear Jesus, help me to do as You ask and try to be good. Help me to listen to my mummy and daddy. Amen

Day 19
Hannah prays

1 Samuel 1 verses 10 and 17

Hannah wanted a baby so she prayed every day. Eli the priest heard Hannah praying.

'Go in peace Hannah,' said Eli the priest to her, 'because the Lord will answer your prayer.'

Talkabout

Do you think that God hears your prayers? Which prayer has He answered for you lately?

Prayer

Dear God, thank You that You hear every prayer I say. Amen

Day 20
Samuel is born

1 Samuel 1 verses 27–28

When the baby was born
Hannah was so thankful to God
for answering her prayers.
'I will call him Samuel,'
she said.
Then Hannah lifted
Samuel up to God because
she knew that Samuel would
serve God as he grew up.

Talkabout

Have you been
thankful to God
recently? What for?

Prayer

Thank You, God,
for answering my
prayers. Amen

Day 21

A special robe

1 Samuel 2 verse 19

Every year, Hannah made Samuel a special robe to wear. Samuel wore it when he went to the Temple to worship God. It was always a very special occasion.

Talkabout

What clothes do you like to wear to church or on any other special day?

Dear God, thank You for Hannah and how she looked after Samuel. Amen

1 Samuel 3 verse 4

A voice calling

One night Samuel was sleeping on the floor of the Temple. He heard a voice calling his name.
'Samuel,' said the voice. Immediately Samuel thought it was Eli the priest calling him.
'I'm here,' he said.

Who do you think was calling Samuel?

Dear God, thank You that You call us by name because You know us so well. Amen

1 Samuel 3 verses 8–10

Day 23
Listen to God

Samuel heard the voice calling him three times. ‘Samuel,’ the voice called. ‘Samuel, Samuel.’

‘It’s God calling you,’ said Eli the priest, ‘and you must listen very carefully to what He tells you.’

Talkabout

How do you think Samuel felt when Eli the priest said this?

Prayer

Dear God, help me to listen to You when You talk to me. Amen

Day 24
God speaks

1 Samuel 3 verse 17

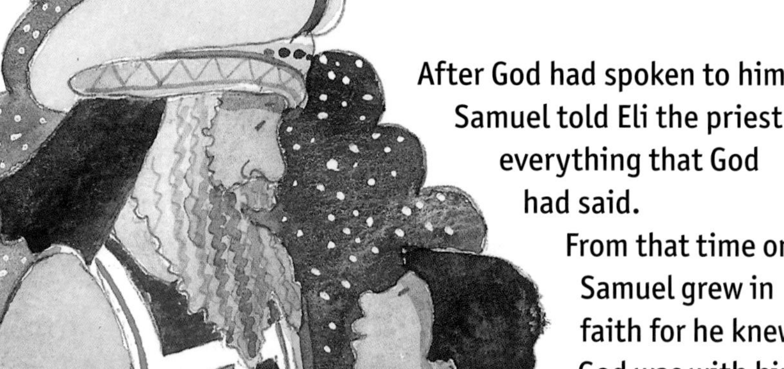

After God had spoken to him, Samuel told Eli the priest everything that God had said.

From that time on Samuel grew in faith for he knew God was with him.

Talkabout

Can you tell somebody if you think that God has spoken to you?

Dear God, thank You that You can speak to people every day. Amen

A FARMER AND HIS SON

Day 25

Luke 15 verses 11–12

Gimme, gimme, gimme

Jesus told the story about a farmer who had two sons. The youngest son wanted his share of the money from the farm.

'Gimme the money,' demanded the son of his father.

Talkabout

'Demanded' means the son didn't ask nicely and he wanted his own way. Have you ever heard someone being demanding and wanting their own way?

Prayer

Please, dear Jesus, help me never to be demanding. Amen

Day 26
Saying goodbye

Luke 15 verse 13

The farmer gave the son his share of the money. Then the son packed his bags and walked away to find a much better life for himself.
His father waved sadly. 'Goodbye, son,' he said, with tears in his eyes.

Talkabout

Have you ever had to say a sad goodbye? Who was it to?

Please, dear Jesus, always be with me when I say a sad goodbye to someone. Amen

Luke 15 verses 13–14 Spend ... spend ... spend!

The son travelled to another country where he spent ALL his money. He bought presents for many friends and also bought lots of silly things. He wasted it all!

Talkabout

What do you think of this son?

Dear Jesus, help me to be very wise when I spend money and not waste it. Amen

Day 28

Luke 15 verses 15–16

What a state!

'Oh no,' wailed the son, 'now I have no money and all my friends have left me and I am sooooo hungry.'
So the son got a job feeding pigs. He hated it!

Talkabout

Why do you think his friends had left him? Were they good friends to have?

Dear Jesus, even though this son did bad things – You still loved him. Thank You. Amen

Unhappy son

Luke 15 verse 17

'I must return home,' said the son. 'This way of living isn't good,' he mumbled. 'My brother and everyone at home have lots to eat ... and I have nothing here at all!'
He was very unhappy.

Talkabout

Have you ever been unhappy? Can you say why?

Prayer

Please, dear Jesus, help me when I am unhappy. Let me know that You are with me in these times. Amen

Luke 15 verse 20

Day 30
Welcome home

The son started to walk back home. He was tired and hungry. His father was looking out of the window and suddenly he saw his young son returning and ran down the pathway to greet him.

'Welcome home, son!' he cried.

Talkabout

Do you like welcoming people when you see them? What do you like to say?

Prayer

Dear Jesus, thank You that You always welcome us with open arms. Amen

Day 31

Repenting son

Luke 15 verse 21

The father hugged and hugged his son. He was so pleased to see him.

'Father,' said the son, 'I've come home to say sorry to you. I also want to say sorry to God because I have behaved so badly.'

Talkabout

Have you had to say sorry recently to someone? What was it for?

Prayer

Dear Jesus, please help me to say sorry to You when I have done something wrong – and to say sorry to the people I may have hurt. Amen

Acts 20 verse 35

It's better to give

David was taking an envelope to church.
'I've put some money in this,' he said to Ben, 'because when I give it I know it will bless some children in Africa who have no food or water. This money will help them.'

Talkabout

To bless means to help someone and make them happy. Who would you like to bless today and why?

Dear Jesus, thank You that You want us to bless other people. Amen

Day 33

Blessed in your house

Deuteronomy 28 verse 6

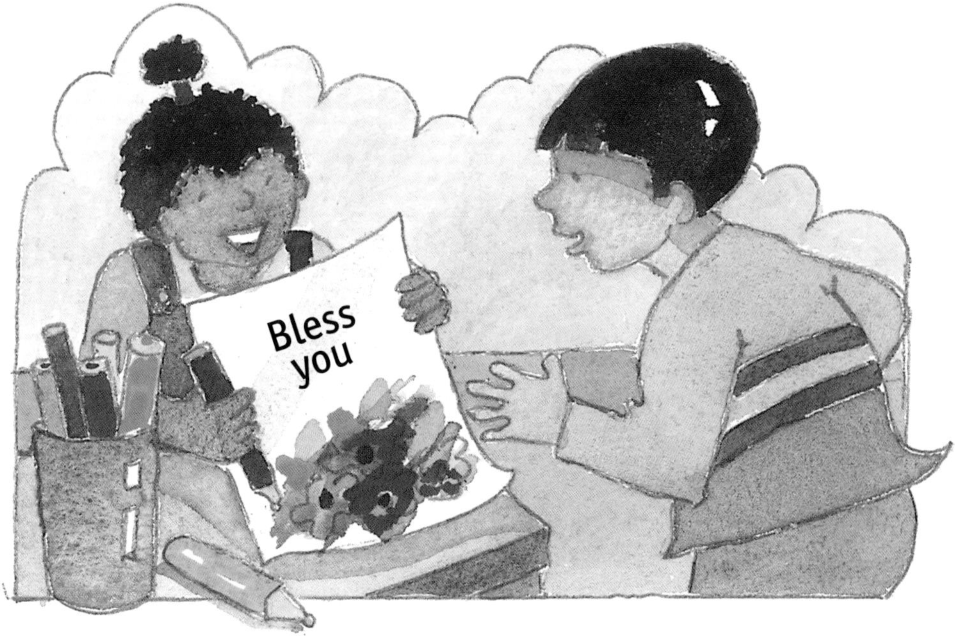

Sarah was colouring in a picture.
'What are you doing?' asked Kim.
'I'm colouring in a picture for our front door,' replied Sarah. 'It says those who come into our house will be blessed.'

Do you like it when friends or family come to your home? Why?

Dear Jesus, thank You that You always want to bless everyone in our home. Amen

Day 34

Psalm 119 verse 2

Blessings from the Bible

David was looking at the pictures in his Bible.
'I really want to know all about Jesus. I want to do the things He tells us to do,' David said to Kim, 'because Jesus wants to bless us.'
'Yes,' agreed Kim, 'I want to learn all about Jesus too.'

Talkabout

Do you like to look at and read your Bible? What do you enjoy when you do this?

Please, dear Jesus, I want to know more about You when I look at and read my Bible. Amen

Psalm 67 verses 5–6

Day 35
God blesses

Max was taking a walk through the park with his daddy. 'WOW!' said Max, 'look, Daddy, at all those birds and butterflies and flowers. Aren't they beautiful!'

'Yes,' said Daddy. 'Isn't it good that God wants to bless us with such wonderful things to look at.'

Talkabout

When you go for a walk what do you like to look at?

Prayer

Dear God, thank You so much for wanting to bless us. Amen

Matthew 25 verse 40

Day 36
Bless someone

'Mummy,' said Kelly, 'can we go to see Grandma? I've drawn this picture and I want to give it to her.'
'Yes,' said Mummy, 'we'll go now, Kelly. I know your picture will bless her.'

Talkabout

What present could you give today that would bless someone?

Prayer

Dear Jesus,
help me to give something today so that someone can be blessed. Amen

Day 37
Bless by helping

Mark 12 verses 29–31

'Sue,' called Mummy, 'I want you to help me. Mr Smith next door isn't well and we need to get some shopping for him. I think it will bless him.'

'Coming Mummy,' replied Sue. They walked together to the shops.

Talkabout

How do you think you can help your neighbours?

Dear Jesus, thank You that You want us to help. Please show me how I can help someone today. Amen

RUTH AND NAOMI

Day 38

Ruth 1 Verse 1

Leaving Bethlehem

A long time ago Naomi, her husband and two sons lived in Bethlehem. But there was no food in the town.

'Let's go to Moab,' said Naomi's husband, 'there's plenty of food there and we would be much better off.'

Talkabout

See if you can look at an atlas to find Bethlehem.

Dear Jesus, help people today looking for food because they don't have any. Amen

Ruth 1 verse 3

Day 39
Left alone

Naomi, her husband and two sons settled in Moab. But something very sad happened. Naomi's husband died.
'Oh dear,' cried Naomi, 'now we are all alone here in Moab.' She was so very upset.

Talkabout

Do you know anyone who is left alone? How could you help them?

Please, dear Jesus, help me to help those people who are alone. Amen

Ruth 1 verse 4

Day 40
Marriage

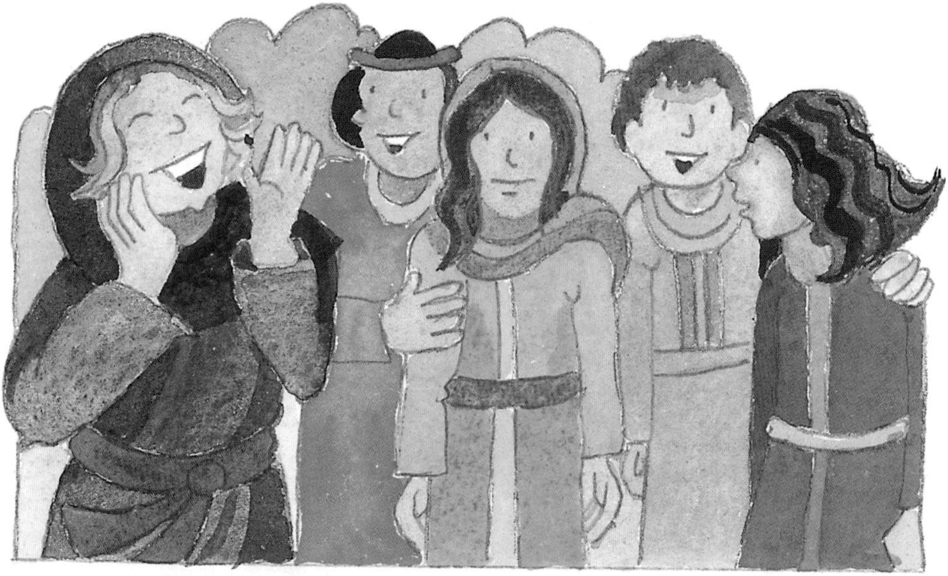

Not long afterwards Naomi's two sons married. One married Orpah and the other married Ruth. This brought comfort to Naomi after her husband had died.

Talkabout

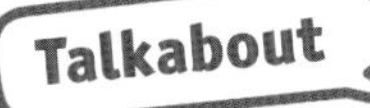

If someone needed comfort how would you comfort them?

Prayer

Dear Jesus, please help me to comfort family and friends who need it. Amen

Ruth 1 verse 5

Day **41**

Even more sad news

After a while something even more sad happened.
Naomi's two sons died.
'Oh no,' wailed Naomi. 'Now we have no one left to take care of us.'

Ruth and Orpah, the two wives, were also very sad. They all cried together.

Talkabout

Can you say how these three women felt during this time?

Dear Jesus, please bring Your comfort into people's lives who have lost someone. Amen

Day **42**

Ruth 1 verses 6 and 15–16

Returning to Bethlehem

During all of this unhappiness Naomi decided to return to Bethlehem. She knew there was food again in Bethlehem.

'I will go with you,' said Ruth to Naomi.

'I will stay here,' said Orpah.

Talkabout

What do you like about Ruth and why?

Dear Jesus, thank You for Ruth as she wanted to be with Naomi on her journey home to Bethlehem. Thank You for her kindness to Naomi. Amen

Day **43**

Ruth works

Ruth 2 verses 2–3

Ruth and Naomi arrived back in Bethlehem. They had no food to eat. A kind farmer called Boaz offered to take care of Ruth and let her pick leftover barley from his fields. Ruth took the barley home to Naomi.

Talkabout What kind of food would you buy to eat?

Dear God, thank You for farmers and farms everywhere who supply us with food. Amen

Ruth 2 verses 14–18

Day 44
Boaz is kind

Boaz made sure Ruth was looked after by his workers as she worked in the fields. They always shared their food with her. He even gave Ruth some barley to take home to Naomi. 'Boaz has been so kind to you, Ruth,' said Naomi.

Talkabout

Who has been kind to you recently?
What did they do?

Dear Lord Jesus, thank You for all the people who have been kind to me. Help me to be kind to other people. Amen

Ruth 3 verses 1–3

Day 45

A special meeting

Naomi wanted Ruth to marry Boaz. She thought that he would be a good husband for Ruth. 'Put on your best clothes for a special meeting with Boaz,' Naomi said to Ruth.

Talkabout

Why do you think Boaz would be a good husband for Ruth? Look at Days 43 and 44.

Thank You, dear Lord, that You knew Boaz would be the right husband for Ruth. Amen

Ruth 4 verse 10

Day 46
A foreigner

However, before Boaz could marry Ruth he had to explain to the local people that Ruth had come from another country. Ruth was a foreigner in Bethlehem.
'I would like Ruth to become my wife,' he said to them.

Talkabout

'Foreigner' means someone from another country. Do you know anyone from another country?

Dear Jesus, help me to be kind to people from other countries. Amen

Ruth 4 verse 13

Day 47
A wedding!

The local people in Bethlehem gave Boaz their blessing. So Boaz married Ruth.

'I am so happy for them,' said Naomi.
The wedding of Boaz and Ruth was very special.

Talkabout

What do you think a wedding should be like?

Thank You, dear Jesus, for those getting married.
Please will You bless them.
Amen

Day 48

A family

Ruth 4 verses 13–16

Later on Ruth gave birth to a son and they called him Obed. Naomi had become a grandmother.

'I'm so blessed,' said Naomi, 'for God has given me a family again after all these years!'

Talkabout

Why did Naomi say this? Look at Days 39 and 41.

Thank You, dear God, that You made Naomi, Ruth and Boaz very happy. Amen

WIND AND WAVES OBEY

Luke 8 verse 22

Sailing with friends

One day Jesus got into a boat with His friends.
'Let's sail over to the other side of the lake,' said Jesus.
It was a beautiful day. So off they all sailed in the boat. The water was very calm.

Talkabout

What do you like to do with your friends?

Dear Jesus, just like You, I enjoy doing things with my friends. Thank You for friends. Amen

Day 50
Fast asleep

Luke 8 verse 23

As the boat sailed away Jesus lay down in the back of the boat. He then fell fast asleep. He was very tired and needed a rest. The boat quietly sailed on.

Talkabout

When do you have a rest? Do you enjoy having a rest?

Prayer

Dear Jesus, it's nice to know that You needed a rest too, just like I do! Amen

Luke 8 verse 23

Day 51
A storm!

Oh dear, suddenly the lake wasn't so peaceful! The wind began to blow across the lake. Dark clouds appeared in the sky and the boat rocked on the very choppy water. A terrible storm had come.

Talkabout

Are you frightened when there's a storm? Or do you like storms?

Dear Jesus, let me know that You are close by when there is a storm. Amen

Luke 8 verse 24

Day 52 Frightened

'Please wake up, Jesus!' cried His friends, 'we are sinking in the lake and we need Your help because we are going to drown!' The friends were in a panic. Jesus woke up and slowly stood up in the boat.

Talkabout

How do you think Jesus' friends felt at this time?

Thank You, Jesus, that even though they were very frightened You were in that boat with Your friends. Amen

Day 53
Command

Luke 8 verse 24

'STOP!' Jesus shouted from the boat, 'You stormy waves and wind – STOP!' And guess what – the storm stopped and the waters became calm again.

Talkabout

How do you think Jesus' friends felt when this happened?

Prayer

Dear Jesus, thank You that You can make stormy seas calm again. Amen

Luke 8 verse 25

Day **54**

Have faith

Jesus looked at His friends. They all looked a bit scared. 'Don't be frightened,' He said to them. 'Why didn't you trust Me? Don't worry, because I am with you all the time.'

Talkabout

Can you say ways that you trust Jesus?

Prayer

Dear Jesus, thank You that You are always with me even when it's stormy. I love You and I trust You. Amen

DON'T BE IMPATIENT

Day 55

Upset waiting

Psalm 37 verse 7

'Where have you been?' yelled David to Kim. 'I've been waiting for you for such a long time to come to my house!' Kim looked at David, 'But I am on time,' he said, 'it's you being impatient!'

Talkabout

'Impatient' means being cross and not waiting. Have you ever been impatient? When?

Dear Jesus, help me not to be impatient with myself or with other people. Amen

Day 56
Hurry up!

1 Thessalonians 5 verse 14

David's grandmother was very old. She had to walk with a walking stick.
'Can't you hurry up, Grandma,' shouted David, 'I want to watch my favourite TV programme!'

Talkabout

Have you ever been impatient with an older person? What happened?

Prayer

Dear Jesus, help me never to be impatient with older people or grandparents. Help me to be kind to them. Amen

Galatians 5 verse 22

Cross and impatient

Kelly was praying quietly.
'Why were you praying, Kelly?' asked Sue when she saw that Kelly had finished praying.
'Because I have just been so cross and impatient with Kim and I needed to say sorry to Jesus,' replied Kelly. 'Now I'm going to say sorry to Kim.'

Talkabout

When you have been impatient with someone have you said sorry to Jesus and to the person?

Prayer

Please, Jesus, help me not to be cross and impatient with anyone. Amen

Day 58
Wait for Jesus

Psalm 37 verse 7

It was holiday time and Daddy wanted Kim and Kelly to have some fun.

'I know,' said Daddy, 'I'm a bit busy today, but tomorrow I'll take you to the swimming pool and you can both splash about in the water!'

Kim looked at his daddy, 'But I want to go today!' he said very loudly.

Talkabout

Have you ever been impatient for something to happen? When?

Prayer

Please, dear Jesus, help me to always wait for the right time and not be impatient. Amen

Day 59

James 1 verse 4

Try, try and try again

Mrs Brown, the playgroup leader, was trying to tell everybody about being good.
David put his hand up. He looked very cross.
'I'm always trying to be good but sometimes I'm not good,' he said.
'Never mind, David,' said Mrs Brown, 'don't be impatient – just try, try and try again.'

Talkabout

Are there times when you find it hard to be good? When are they?

Dear Jesus, help me not to be cross and let me always try to be good. Amen

Romans 12 verse 12

Day 60
Prayer helps

'Why are you looking so happy, David?' asked Sarah.
'Because,' said David, 'I've just prayed to Jesus to help me not to be impatient and I believe He's heard my prayer and He's going to help me!'

Talkabout Does it make you happy when you know that Jesus has heard your prayer and has helped you to do something? Can you say what it was?

Prayer Thank You, dear Jesus, for always helping me when I pray and for teaching me to be patient. Amen

Three more beautifully illustrated daily devotionals by Eira Reeves, for 3- to 6-year-olds:

£5.99 each

ISBN: 978-1-85345-518-6

ISBN: 978-1-85345-519-3

ISBN: 978-1-85345-545-2

For when you're too old for Jesus and Me Every Day

Topz helps 7- to 11-year-olds get to know God and His Word through an exciting, day-by-day look at the Bible. Daily Bible readings and simple prayers are augmented by readers' contributions along with fun and colourful word games, puzzles and cartoons.

£13.80 UK annual subscription (6 issues)
Individual copies also available: £2.49 each
72-page, full-colour booklet, 210x148mm, published bimonthly
ISSN: 0967-1307

Visit **www.cwr.org.uk** or call **01252 784710**

Prices correct at time of printing.